PLANTED & PRODUCING

by

Jameka D. Anderson, MBA

Anointed Writers Publishing
Portmore, Jamaica

Printed on demand

ISBN: 978-976-96398-2-9

Book Cover Design by LogoMePlease

Published by:
Anointed Writers Publishing
Portmore, Jamaica
www.theanointedwriter.com

To my parents:

Thank you for loving me and encouraging me to never settle for less.

Love, Meka

CONTENTS

INTRODUCTION

Have you ever felt like the place you are currently assigned to is limiting your potential? For some of us that place is our job. While, for others, it can be church. I'm sure you have said to yourself on various occasions: "What is the purpose of me being here?" It is a frustrating and discouraging place to be in. However, a question like this one is a natural and honest one to ask. After all, we are human.

The purpose of this book isn't to throw a virtual pity party nor to give you ammunition to host your own. It is to challenge your thinking and develop your perspective. Consider that there are gifts deep down within you that will help someone else. You are the answer to someone else's prayer but God wants you in your current position to mold, change and develop you.

After reading this book, I want you to

focus on the assignment regardless of the circumstances. You may feel planted in the environment, but that doesn't mean that you are dormant. It is time to get busy and begin bearing fruit from your God-given assignment.

Throughout this book you will identify where you are, learn about a few people who were in your shoes, and use their lives as a guide to shift your mindset to help you stay focused on your current assignment.

Let's dive in.

PLANTED & PRODUCING

"Being planted usually has a negative connotation. However, your view depends on how you choose to align your perspective."
- Jameka Anderson

CHAPTER ONE: PLANTED? WHAT'S THAT?

When you are planted you are placed or fixed in a specified position for a particular purpose. That suggests that in order to be planted in your current position you would have had to be placed by your own efforts or by someone or something else. Here's a simple example of being planted: It's Christmas time and at your place of employment your supervisor is suggestively requesting assistance with planning the Christmas events. You feel compelled to offer assistance so you do. After suggesting a brilliant theme and idea, your supervisor appoints you as lead coordinator.

Before you continue, take some time to reflect on the questions below as your pruning exercise:

How do you feel about being planted in a position and not agreeing with the placement?

How do you handle being planted in a position that is uncomfortable?

Do you think it is okay to abruptly remove yourself?

When planted in an uncomfortable position, do you remain stagnant and begin to despise your assignment?

I bet these are tough questions to answer. We all have been in positions that we would rather not be in. It is all a part of our life as human beings. Though these emotions are innate, they are not a free pass to get stuck or be stagnant.

Can you imagine where we would be if Jesus Christ of Nazareth had decided to pick up and relocate from Jerusalem and head to America instead? Yes, I know it would have been impossible at the time but I am trying to make a point - work with me. If Jesus didn't remain planted in position to complete his assignment on earth specifically how God had intended, then billions of people wouldn't have received salvation. Our obedience to being planted is simply a fraction of the bigger picture of our lives. As our Lord and Savior did, we must deny ourselves, pick up our crosses, and follow Him.

When you accept Jesus Christ as your Lord and Savior, your job is now to submit your free will to Him to do the work He has called you to do. And, sometimes that means being planted in places that don't feel that great or purposeful. In its initial stages when you say yes to Christ and begin to experience the newness of salvation, you feel loved and special. As the journey continues, and you are filled with the Holy Spirit, you begin to realize that giving up your will isn't as easy. You must align your decisions to the ones He desires for you to make. When you want to move out of position you feel a nudge (conviction) that keeps you in check. In my own walk with God, I have learned that on the journey, you will end up in interesting predicaments orchestrated by Him simply for His glory to be shown through you. These situations continuously test you so that you are displaying characteristics that communicate that you belong to Him.

I want you to be honest with yourself about where your heart posture is. Once you begin to have honest conversations about where you are, it becomes easier to communicate your cares to God. God is so abundant in love, grace, and mercy. Focusing your heart on God will cause you to realize that the process of being planted isn't so bad. The reality is, we all will be planted somewhere for a specific season. We just have to make a conscious effort to remember that we are doing it for God's glory. 1 Peter 2:16 says, "Act as free men, and do not use your freedom as a covering for evil, but use it as bondslaves of God." When you choose to be planted in places out of your obedience to God, there is a sense of freedom that you can acknowledge because you know that being connected to Him doesn't keep you in evil bondage.

Thought: You may be planted somewhere with the right perspective or you may have taken some time to get the perspective right. Let's take a moment to be honest about it. How has being in that place affected you? Were you excited at first? Have you begun to despise your purpose? I'm giving you room to open your heart to God about these things.

Prayer: Father, I'm thankful that you have a purpose for me. I'm thankful that you decided to use me as an instrument to have your purpose accomplished in the earth. Sometimes I lose sight of why you may have planted me here. So, give me the strength to withstand all tests and trials in Jesus' Name, Amen.

"God wants you to remain focused on your assignment which is bigger than any day to day task."
– Jameka Anderson

CHAPTER TWO:
I DARE YOU TO BE BOLD!

Since you aren't journeying through this alone, I'm going to be transparent about a situation that I'm currently going through so that you can empathize with me. In 2017, I obtained a new job that set me on a more marketable career path. I thought this was great because I felt overlooked and unappreciated at the previous place of employment; even though this new job didn't come with an instant increase in my annual salary. I knew that the work processes were different, but I didn't think it would be a challenge to get used to since the overall idea of the work is the same. Man, when I got there, things appeared to be so behind on the technological side of things, and it frustrated my millennial self so badly.

It's been two and a half years later and I'm still employed there. I've been tried, tested, and promoted. I've actually searched for other job opportunities and received offers but nothing seemed to work out. I tried my best to think positively but I had days where I would have thoughts like, "Wow, why does God still want me here?" I truly believe He wants me to remain focused on my assignment that is bigger than my day to day tasks. He allowed me to be there to serve under leadership to advise them on new, fresh strategies. I've gained a ton of experience in a leadership capacity because my boss trusts me to meet with directors often regarding assistance with their needs. These are all skills that are necessary. They even aid in how I serve at my local church. My boss often tells me how I also bring her a sense of peace because I'm able to calm her down when emotions get high when dealing with our coworkers. If I were to be so selfish and only focused on me, and my needs it would be hard to accurately seek God on how I am to serve others.

I would be lying if I said I get this right every day because I don't. I am a work in progress just like the next person. I want to encourage you to know that where you are now isn't where you will be five years from now.

Pause...make sure you don't take that literally.

This simply means that your perspective will change somewhere along the line. While you wait for the platforms and "big" opportunities, God wants your submission to Him to be intact so that you aren't tossed to and fro during the challenging seasons in your life. Luke 16:10 says, "If you are faithful in little things, you will be faithful in large ones. But if you are dishonest in little things, you won't be honest with greater responsibilities." How can God trust you with more if you aren't being faithful where you are right now? It's easier said than done, but you must strive to have this perspective daily. I love the phrase "If you can't say amen, then say ouch." Me, currently: OUCH!

Right now, I am planted at this job until God says otherwise and you are where you are until God sees it fit to change the circumstance. This can be in any type of situation of life. However, you cannot abandon your current assignments simply because you are uncomfortable with your circumstances.

Thought: It's time for you to be BOLD. Take some time to think about a situation you are in right now that you cannot simply walk away from. Be honest about it. Pour out to God right here in this moment and let Him know about your frustrations. Ask Him for guidance on how you can be able to see things from His perspective. Don't hesitate to ask Him for the grace to remain committed to the work even though the circumstances are difficult.

Feel free to use this prayer below as a guide:

Prayer: Father, I thank you for placing me where I am. Forgive me for complaining about the negative aspects of where I am, and give me the strength to see the good in this uncomfortable situation. In Jesus' Name, Amen.

Jameka D. Anderson

"A residual benefit that
comes out of the testing is
growth in your endurance."
– Jameka Anderson

CHAPTER THREE:
PLANTED FOR PURPOSE

Let me introduce you to an amazing woman of wisdom. She is from Bethlehem in Judah and she is a wife with two sons. She is headed to Moab with her family, and once they arrive, she loses her husband and both sons. She's connected with her daughters-in-law, and all three of them are now widows. One by the name Orpah decides to return to her family. The other one, Ruth, decides to go with her mother-in-law back to her hometown. Her name, is Naomi which means "pleasantness" but she wasn't in the most pleasant situation.

Naomi usually gets referenced only because of Ruth's faithfulness but it's easy to overlook her story since it doesn't seem as pleasant as Ruth's. When they returned to Naomi's hometown, I can imagine how difficult it must have been. She has moved on with her life and her family, just to return to what she always knew. Not only that; she has to stay there planted in Bethlehem.

The beauty in this story is not that she was planted; but she was planted for a bigger purpose. She was to play a greater role in God's plan. Who knew that she would be a key instrument in mentoring and teaching Ruth what to do and how to carry herself so that she could become married to Boaz? Not only that, she would become one of the matriarchs in the lineage of Jesus. How cool is that! Yet, if Naomi decided to stay bitter and not focus on tending to Ruth, she could have missed the opportunity to realize how God was arranging things. Naomi even had the opportunity to nurse Ruth's child, Obed.

I wanted to share an example of someone being planted in an unpleasant circumstance to demonstrate how we can still be used by God. Sometimes the things we experience are just trials and tests to make us stronger. James 1:3 says, "For you know that when your faith is tested, your endurance has a chance to grow." This scripture is paramount because it encourages us to go through the tests knowing that God is there and He is in control. We also have some residual benefits that come out of our testing which is growth in our endurance. This endurance is a testimony for someone else. Your endurance can be the blueprint for someone else's path.

Thought: Can you recall a time when you were in an uncomfortable spot, yet someone else was blessed because of it? How did it make you feel?

Prayer: Father, sometimes I don't understand the circumstances I am in. It may be because of my own disobedience or because you are trying to perfect something in me. Your word says that Your ways are not my ways, and Your thoughts are not my thoughts. So, Lord, please help me to be at peace with the unknown. Also, Lord, help me to remain submitted in my assignments given by You so that I can help someone else. In Jesus' Name. Amen

"Allow him to perfect you,
prune you and purge you so that
you start looking like Jesus Christ. "
– Jameka Anderson

CHAPTER FOUR:
I CAN PRODUCE HERE

We have examined what it means to be planted and we've come to grips with the benefits. Now, let's get to the producing portion. Realizing where you are and having the strength and energy to produce can be challenging. I have my moments when I don't feel like doing anything because the circumstances don't fit what I want at the moment. Yet, I don't have the luxury to sit back on the work that's set out for me to accomplish. I'm encouraging you to do the same. Don't allow where you currently are to hinder you from being productive. Don't allow yourself to wither and dry up because you don't feel fulfilled. There are people that need you and the gifts that are on the inside of you! I am often reminded of a question I heard at a conference 3 years ago. The pastor asked, "What is on the other side of your obedience?" I don't listen to this reminder like I should, but when I do I am reminded that I am not here on earth existing just for me. We all were placed here to help someone else regardless of us liking where we are or not.

Take Joseph for example; Joe for short. He had an interesting life story and it amazes me every time I read about him. Joe was placed in some unique predicaments such as slavery, working for an Egyptian officer. He was even thrown into prison for something he did not do. Throughout his life, Joe was planted in these places by God to be sure that his potential manifested. All the unpleasant moments he endured shaped him to be the second in command to the Pharaoh at that time.

Let's pause for a second...

It is so difficult to wrap our heads around what God allows to happen to us for the sake of His promises coming to pass. Joseph had to go through rejection, abandonment, lies being told on him and so much more.

Yet, it made him the biblical champion that we know him as today. God still allowed his story to be recognized as a true example of redemption. While Joseph was in these predicaments, he still worked! He didn't throw a temper tantrum, nor did we see him complain to God about why he was where he was. He continued to do as he was instructed to do by God and by his authority figures in all phases. Man... this takes strength! Can you imagine being lied on and rejected and having to continue serving where you are like nothing happened? Maybe this has happened to you. I would like to challenge your perspective. What matters more to you? Is it what people are saying and doing to you? Or, is it what God is saying and doing through you?

When we receive salvation through Jesus Christ, this doesn't make us exempt from natural human interaction. Where there are humans, you will have all types of issues. However, you cannot allow your conditions to halt your progression or your production. If Joseph didn't tend to the needs of Potiphar's house with excellence the story would have a different ending. Refer to Genesis 39. He would have never gained the experience to be able to rule over Egypt as second in command. And what if he never worked on hearing God correctly and speaking when the Lord gave him the permission to do so. He wouldn't have interpreted the dreams of the cupbearer that ultimately led to his freedom from prison.

I know that you may not be in a situation that is favorable but I pray that you are able to shift your perspective to see things differently. You can use this time to allow God to help you with personal development. Seek Him on what is or should be a priority at the moment. Don't allow yourself to be too overwhelmed. Allow him to perfect you, prune you and purge you so that you start looking like Jesus Christ in your own life. To my non-Christian readers, focus on your faith and attempt to apply the principles to your situation.

Thought: Think of ways that you can begin to work on your self-development and the things you can produce in the uncomfortable spaces in your life.

Prayer: Lord, I thank you for placing me in a position that can bring me closer to you.

Please teach me how to look at things from your perspective. Help me to see why you placed me here and I pray that you provide guidance on how I need to produce where I am. In Jesus' Name. Amen.

"A residual benefit that comes out of the
testing is growth in your endurance."
– Jameka Anderson

CHAPTER FIVE:
ACTIVATION TIME

We have come to the end of the book y'all. Though a short-read, it makes me happy to know that you stuck with me through it all. My purpose for this book was to originally have it in an eBook format only but the plans changed. I want you to know that I am proud of you for where you have been and where you are going! No more time to waste. It is now time to get to work! Activate! Before we close out, I would like to share a little bit about my journey with you. I hope that you are encouraged by this:

In the summer of 2019, I had my world turn upside down. I appeared to be in good spirits but things were coming together and falling apart all at the same time. I serve as the Chief Financial Officer of The GIFTED

Network and we were planning our first prophetic summit in Jamaica. I was also the Maid of Honor in my best friend's wedding. My full-time job had been extremely busy and my finances were all over the place. Oh, and the icing on the cake was having to abruptly move from my home and having to downsize into an apartment. I had no clue whether I was going or coming. My prayer life was non-existent and I got back into terrible habits that included seeking validation from men. With all that was happening simultaneously, my business Anderson Advisory Services, was the last thing on my mind. However, when I arrived in Jamaica at our summit, the business was the very thing that God decided to speak to me about.

As a business owner, leader, or whatever role you may play, sometimes you are planted in different mindsets and physical places that seem to be like a dead end. I didn't realize that I had allowed my external circumstances to place me in an unproductive mindset. When things aren't growing at the rate you desire, it can be a bit discouraging. If you're a business owner you may wonder if things are ever going to be better. You may wonder if you will ever own your own building or be able to hire employees to carry the load. The answer is yes but it will come with time. Right now, you simply can't despise small beginnings. If you are planted in a season of operating your business on your couch, continue to produce those business tasks there. If you are planted on your job and you feel overlooked, continue to produce your very best work there. I hope you're catching the drift. We cannot allow where we are today to overshadow where we can be in the future. It's imperative for us to ground ourselves, take control of our thoughts, accept where we are, and find the opportunity to produce and prosper wherever we may be. This opens the door for gratitude and gratefulness once you expand!

I don't know what your religion is, but God can speak to you through various channels. God spoke to me on one of the days of our summit regarding the life of my business. Prophetic words truly bring insight and wisdom to what God is thinking regarding your current situation. The apostle who spoke to me encouraged me, brought clarity, and gave me hope for the future of my business. He literally called me and my business by name! If I had a way of playing the video for you through this book, I would. It still blows my mind how detailed this prophetic word was. I truly thought that God had forgotten about me because I was so busy taking care of everything and everyone else. Yet, he used the apostle to speak to me about my business. This gave me the fuel that I needed to come home and reinvest my time into my business. I had to go back to God and sit at His feet to see where He wanted me to go.

I'm still not where I want to be with my business, but through prayer, patience, and persistence I am very well on my way to where I believe God wants me to go. I wanted to share a broken area with you to remind you that it is okay to take a step back and analyze where you currently are. Take some time to realize what's going on around you and reassess your priorities. Sometimes, our businesses are unproductive because we are being too productive in other areas. There are times where we have to pause and recalibrate so that we are offering our best to our clients and customers.

You may be able to relate to my situation or you may have something completely different going on with you. However, I want to reassure you that you are okay. It is not the end of the world if you don't post that new graphic. It's ok if you forgot to reply to an email or if you dropped the ball on your t-shirt launch. If your body is filled with pain and you have no energy to do a task today that's alright. Life happens. You don't have to let it overwhelm you. The scripture that helps me to rest is 1 Peter 5:7 which says "Give all your worries and cares to God because He cares for you." Sometimes we can get stuck in the bad side of current situations to the point where we forget to rely on God so that He can produce the necessary fruit out of us.

I didn't allow my circumstances in life to stop me from running my business. So, I am encouraging you to hang in there. You may have moments where you don't understand what is going on; and have moments that seem dry and uncertain. These are the best times to seek God so that you can watch Him work a miracle through you and in your business.

The remainder of this chapter will be dedicated to some affirmations that you will read aloud; and a prayer that will encourage you in your current circumstances.

Affirmations:

"God has a plan for me, and no matter how long it takes it will be a plan for a future and a hope" (Jeremiah 29:11)

"God sees me and He knows each and everything that I need" (Genesis 16:14)

"God is the supplier of ALL of my needs" (Philippians 4:19)

"I can do all things through Christ who gives me strength (Philippians 4:13)

"God will never leave me nor forsake me, no matter how difficult a circumstance may be" (Hebrews 13:5)

"Abba will perfect the things that concern me, he cares about me and his mercy endures forever with me" (Psalm 138:8)

"I am safe with God, because his name all by itself is a strong fortress for me" (Proverbs 18:10)

"I know that God has given me strength, but His strength is made perfect when I'm weak. This reminds me that I'm not fighting alone." (2 Corinthians 12:9)

"God is abundant in grace, so He will provide enough grace for the tasks He has called me to" (2 Corinthians 12:9)

"Even in the uncomfortable situations, I know that God can use it to work out for my good" (Romans 8:28)

Prayer: Father, I thank you for the person who is reading this book right now. I thank you for the destiny that you have set ahead of them. I thank you for the time and diligence it has taken for them to read and finish this book. I don't know what their current circumstances are but I do know that you are the God who sees and knows all. This lets me know that you are aware of every need, as well as every trial and test that they must endure. I pray that the tests don't make their faith in you waiver. I pray that they remain planted, just as the tree you described in Psalm 1 so that they bring fruit in and out of season. I pray that they don't allow anxiety and frustration to distract them. I pray that they have Godly community around them to strengthen them when they feel weak. I pray that they run to you as their fortress for rest when they are weary. Give them the strength not to give up in their weary moments because there are so many things you have in store of them. I thank you and I pray that they hang in there and bloom where they are planted. In Jesus' Name, Amen!

Now, go grow...